GW00634466

The Nervous Flyer's Companion

Gráinne Tobin

SUMMER PALACE PRESS

First published in 2010 by

Summer Palace Press
Cladnageeragh, Kilbeg, Kilcar, County Donegal, Ireland
and
31 Stranmillis Park, Belfast BT9 5AU

LOTTERY FUNDED

Printed by Nicholson & Bass Ltd.

A catalogue record for this book is available from the British Library

ISBN 978-0-9560995-8-7

FSC

Mixed Sources
Product group from well-managed
forests, controlled sources and
recycled wood or fibre
Cert no. SGS-COC-005221
www.fsc.org
© 1996 Forest Stewardship Council

This book is printed on elemental chlorine-free paper

for
Andy Carden

Acknowledgments

Some of the poems in this book have previously been published in: *Cyphers, The Dickens, Fortnight, Irish Feminist Review, Ulla's Nib* and the *Mourne Observer.*

'The Universalismo Teapot' will be in the forthcoming issue of *Poetry Ireland Review* edited by Paul Muldoon.

Three poems have been exhibited: *Callan* on Derry Central Library's Poet Tree; *The Process* in the Old Museum Arts Centre and *In The Museyroom* in the Pitt Rivers Museum in Oxford.

Biographical Note

Gráinne Tobin was brought up in Armagh and now lives and works in Newcastle, County Down, where she is a founder-parent and teacher in Shimna Integrated College. She is a member of the Word of Mouth poetry collective, and a contributor to the Word of Mouth anthology (Blackstaff 1996), which was translated into Russian and published in St Petersburg. She has produced English versions of poems by the St Petersburg poet Galina Gamper for Word of Mouth's current parallel text project. She is the author of a previous Summer Palace collection, *Banjaxed* (2002).

CONTENTS

Migrant

Tell me a really story. Tell me what it was like
when you were small, which way you walked to school,
the garden where you tried to dig to the other side of the world,
your uncle's rows of leafy plants to eat,
the orchard tree you climbed to hide,
the old lady waving from the window, the bags of coloured sweets
and the house you were told you'd inherit.

Apricots and lemons.
If you go there, pick some for me.

Tierhogar, Spelga, Qatamon.
The names are spells.

When you shovelled soil aside with your scaled-down spade,
did you know you'd come out where you are now?
That your children would save cereal boxes
to reconstruct your home in sticky-tape and cardboard?

Tell me what happened. Exactly.

Here and There

When we went south in summer to God's own country
where Grandfather lived, the engine blew smuts
and my mother washed my face with spit.
Away was fixed beyond Cuchulainn's Gap,
on the other side of the mountain.

The sleepers were sold long ago.
At six years old they took me to the station
to see the last train leave:
Something to tell your grandchildren.

Aeroplanes take my parents' grandchildren
shooting off cleanly into the sky: school trips
to snowy ranges where they ski, hot cities
ready to be photographed. *Away*
is further and not so far; miles multiply
on maps but the family voice comes over
the phone line into the old house.

Children from the lanes of meadowsweet
picnic on Californian beaches,
where the Miwoks told their stories
before the Jesuits and the smallpox came.
Wild yellow lupins scent their headland.
Thoughts burst from pods,
seeds carried in a trouser cuff,
windborne across continents.

Landed, tracking the eastern coast,
the map dog's rough spine,
on the Enterprise Express we roll past harbours,
seagulls, inlets, painted boats, lighthouses like toys,
with the low growl of the train's wheels
below us, heartbeat and pulse, swaying and rocking.

From the blond hayfield done up in curlers
for harvest, black crows rise.
Five poplars steady the horizon. A Norman tower
stands in a cut field like a lone horse.
Brick platforms of Empire pose
in a florescence of fern.
The Cooley Ridge. We're pushing north
past dry-stone walls,
Scots pines and thorn bushes,
along the serrated line on the wall-map
where the island meets its sea.

Happy Days in Sunny Newcastle

The air's washed now,
last night's sad leavings
swept up and away.
Van drivers park outside the bakery
with fried eggs held in breakfast soda farls.

Arcades of slot machines
lie berthed between streams
that slip downhill to a tideline flagged with pebbles,
faded wood, wrecked loot, rubber gloves, broken glass
abraded to droplets by the tumbling waves.

The daily walker on his coatless course
between youth and age,
observing wading birds and children's games.

Up for a trip, out for a drive,
dandering down the promenade.

Loudhailer hymns, crusaders' tracts
warn of strange temptations
offered to ice-cream lickers,
candy-floss lovers.

In the chip-shops' wake the street
opens to the sea
which is the reason for everything,
shingle bank,
shops and houses,
foundations sunk in marsh,
confined by a shadowed arm
where mountains lift out of the water,
growing darkness like moss
over the forest where the young
roost with beer and campfires.

Heron pacing the harbour at twilight
stiff-collared in clerical grey,
squinting at coloured lights
edging the bay.

Far out, the lighthouse signalling,
Good - night
chil - dren.

Unbelievable

All the most unbelievable things
are the ones that turn out to be true.
Babies come out of people.
Governments disobey their own laws.

Gypsies sing to the rising moon
in defence bunkers by the ferryport,
where ladybirds swarm on your orange tent.
You zip yourself inside reading *Nausea*.

The woman at the Poste Restante takes pity
on your last coin, gives you both envelopes:
a card enclosing the fare home, a letter
with news of the latest political murders.

The Process

Hope again: the backpack's bulk
released from dented shoulders,
impacted spine and splayed-out feet
that keep the pressure and the shape
of overload.

Until you straighten up
it hardly hurts at all.
Then bruises colour in, that frostbite nip,
numbed muscles ache and sting.
Each forward step is suffered like a loss.

Left foot, strawfoot, persisting in our stride,
dunting along head-down into the wind,
we dream of dancing 'til at last
in one of history's aftermaths,
the pulse returns,
our music starts to play.

Elizabeth Told Me

Elizabeth pinned roses on her dress,
and lady searchers at the prison
poured tea in china cups with saucers.

The bridegroom could not keep from staring.
Forbidden metal,
he turned the bright teaspoon in his fingers.

She slipped him some roses,
a covert operation,
their first touch.

At her next visit he said
every man in the wing had slept
with a rose petal under his pillow.

Farewell to the Road

Feeding the car between high hawthorn hedges,
channels in drumlin fields of sheep and whins,
unravelling seasons spooling out behind.

Down the Devil's Elbow, patched with heather,
wheels roll out tarmac like a length of cloth
stitched by machine, threading kilometres.

Over the Bann in a bubble, morning and evening,
to pause in traffic by stone polar bears
raised to the trials of the North West Passage.

Years of drive-time news repeated at the bridge.
Alone and listening, braking, tripped by tears,
watching for these humans who survive.

They take their daily places on the verges
like figures on an ornamental clock,
signing the time, through bud and leaf-fall.

Farm-gate woman with her fodder bucket,
limping girl out for a difficult walk,
old man in a hat, saluting the car with his stick.

Two headscarved sisters passing the church, in step,
young and solemn in older women's raincoats,
eyes on guard in sixteenth-century faces.

Leaning at evening into the pedal, swinging
the car uphill to the moment of pleasure,
the returning glimpse of farmhouse, nissen hut,

door in fresh gloss red, and the full washing line,
swelling the wind's ceremonial dance
against a big domed sky, before the curve

swoops to raise the blind on Donard.

A Postcard to Dulcie September

First-ever taste of South African red,
when the boycott was lifted,
like sipping blood. Too late to tell you.

After the election we drank a toast
in Cape Pinotage robust as you had been
in England fifteen years before,
with your big laugh, your tall bones,
that high round squeezy ass
you said your Hottentot granny left you.

You were nowhere by then; five bullets finished it;
but I still want to say, remember when
both of us saw that bully off, who thought
he'd lead our women's liberation group?
And the time you couldn't make me learn
your exy-ozy Xhosa language click?

Five prison years, and five in house-arrest:
you hoarded joy, schooled yourself to seize
all happiness within your reach,
refusing to co-operate with pain.

We find your name on websites, for our son.
It's on a school in France, two public squares.
The list of assassins is pages long.

I see you at the Paris bureau door,
the morning's mail held ready in your hand.
Your killer's rifle stifles all reports –
a silencer, translated from the French.

My postcard, never sent, falls to the ground.

Internal Exile

It was all too much. He took to his bed,
and stayed there for ten years,
begetting, however, several more children.
She carried trays up and down the stairs
and he lay hidden, staring out to sea.
At night he watched the lighthouse
winking through his shuttered window.
All the money was gone. It didn't matter.
They picked a living from their children's labour
at this salty edge of earth, where
there was always fishing, chickens,
a smallholding of sorts, some barter.

What got him up and dressed at last was this.
One afternoon from under his eiderdown
he gazed beyond the glass panes, as the waves,
framed by floral curtains, silently rose,
and gulped his two sons in their boat –
corpses never found, skiff washed ashore in pieces,
the coastal searches just as futile
as that warm sanctuary where the need
to witness woke him in the end.

The Universalismo Teapot

From kitchen windowsill between spider plant and coffee jug
let's raise the shiny two-cup teapot bought below the Alhambra
on a day when home-made banners flew from the windows of Granada
saying NO TO THE WAR among geraniums and bicycles.

Embossed in Arabic with who knows what homely epigrams,
A Present From Al Andaluz, perhaps, or *God is Good, Don't Worry*,
it may give us a handle on events, or buffing its gleam rub a genie
to grant our wishes while we drink more tea and read the paper.

The bearded man who sold it was all soul and handshakes, scooping
an extra couple into the jingling shop to raise an eager toast
the joy of French and Irish taking their ease to choose
domestic pleasures, blushing over phrasebooks in a time of armies.

No wine, he knew we'd understand, calling for apple juice
and a tray of gilded glasses, pouring a ceremonial chalice
for the strangers, smiling into our faces as if to embrace us,
brimming over to explain the word he wanted – Universalismo.

Two Old Men in Primetime

1. The Pragmatist

The Catholic grocer of Lodz,
happy to sell his parsnips and potatoes
for wedding rings handed through barbed wire.

That's life, that's how things are. They had to do it.
Of course we did get richer. Nothing can change,
or you will hang with them as the proverb says.

Someone in the editing suite insisted
on voice-over matched with nightmare montage,
lollystick limbs of the ghetto's half-dead children.

The talking grocer's old, his answer settled,
but watch his eyes slide from this picture,
his world as it is and ever shall be amen.

2. MacNamara in Fog

The ex-secretary of state for war
thinks more than ever that killing
human beings is to be avoided.

See his eyelids flicker at decisions
enforced in haste, mistaking enemies'
diplomacy or vanity or error.

Close-up in keen detail, the things he knows
he now at times regrets. Numbers of lives
spilt in confusion. Tears for only one.

More luck than judgement is a rule he's learned.
His death comes now into the viewfinder.
Age-spotted hands remember blood.

Scabies, 1970.

The whole town knew someone in the prison –
pinpoints of blood on the children's sheets
were not from hives or the strawberry harvest.

Our mother, mortified!

My new English boyfriend
on his first visit home to meet my family
shared the jar of petrol emulsion
we brush-stroked on each other's seamless bodies,
interning the mites that burrowed under warm skin,
suffocating their insurgent itch,
sealing their tunnels with poisoned residue.

His scarified torso, the unclean stigmata
we couldn't explain to his parents.

Old sores on both our houses.

Girls Who Tell Stories
for Maria Bernada Sobeirons of Lourdes

In a cathedral town
in a disputed province
before puberty and riots
we had piety for homework.

In the decades of the rosary
when we lived behind the world
before we saw our homes on TV news
every family kept blessed water
in hollow statues of the virgin Mary
brought from Lourdes by pilgrims
and female children scanned the skies
longing for prophecies
for secrets to be heard.

Our days becalmed in the dry gaps where cattle crossed
between thorn hedges by the puddling river

we scraped at mudbanks for the holy fountain
believing the springs of life flowed past our houses.

Was it any wonder
we thought the covering cloud would part and light burst through
from the back of beyond
the lovely young lady
sister
little mother
her sunrayed fingertips
her whitest robe
her skyblue belt
her yellow roses.

Now I'm emptying Lourdes water down the sink
as the vision bubbles from a new source.

In the hilly back-country
of an earlier century
in an overlooked province
of a rallying nation
children are sent out in winter
collecting bones and fallen twigs on icy paths.

The girl does not speak the French we learned at school
is not wearing traditional costume
will not appear in a Hollywood film
and her name is not Bernadette Soubirous.

Breath stings her throat
grabs her thin ribs
keeps her from stepping with the others
across the frozen water.

She's wrapped up wheezing on the dirt floor of the cave
where the sheep she minds take shelter in bad weather
not as foul as the room where they all sleep
her father back from jail
her mother who does bits of jobs to feed them
herself the only daughter
her three brothers
the souls of five dead children
the prayers that each birth would be the last.

She's small for fourteen
unschooled
hired out for labour
and now that her blood has come
her bare scabbed feet
plant her forever in this soil
but she holds within her vision
the shining girl who visits her
who speaks her language
and shows her where to find a well of clear bright health.

Word leaks out and Bernadeta
is followed by strangers
threatened and questioned
photographed in clean clothes
and postcards are sold of her beauty
so the nuns take her in
to work as hard as before
tending the sick in their infirmary
and after telling the sisters about it just the once
she's forbidden to explain herself ever again.

My Father Invites me to Contribute to the Church

My coffee-plunger tilts
under the awkward question,
misfires, skites a Roman candle
of scalding grit and steam,
coming down like a ton of gunpowder
on the unguarded arm,
avoiding an answer.

Pinned down for its own good
under the splashing tap,
insulted flesh refuses to ignore
the implications: swells, blisters,
flings up skin in a puffed-out gesture
of choking rage, a liquid-
filled dome, at once numbed
and ringing with the high held note of alarm.

The dressing is so large it's comical,
but underneath, ripped-up meat
frightens the children and has to be covered,
while cell after cell is soothed, made good
by Mother Nature in her lab coat
whispering *it doesn't matter, never mind,*
he didn't mean it like that.

Over long weeks the roughness shrinks away
and the raw torn place
starts new like the petals of a flower,
no problem, no questions asked.

Once Burned

Nudging the hot towel-rail,
      stung skin dissolves, whitens,
sags like wet muslin.

      A waterproof patch
seals the arm's leaking surface,
      an overflow valve
for backed-up tears.

      The body is not
listening to reason,
      but pulls itself together,
drawing a membrane
      across the red wound,
replacing absent layers
      with thicker skin.

The bandage peels off,
      a neat, pale oblong.
Take care.

Mortal Sin

Hidden between next door's fence and coalshed
the child reaches up to squeeze the first stolen pod,
cutting with a thumbnail along the scored edge,
pulling the stalk-string fastening,
exposing tiny peas lined up in rows,
the slotted teeth of a hairslide,
sherbety pats of fresh green –
and eats her fill, an Eve in Eden.

Grown to the age of reason and her first confession,
she runs into clean air like a sheet
drying in the wind of absolution.

The Amorous Motorway

'The M6 contains 2.5 million pulped Mills and Boon novels.
The books are used as a sound absorber
and to hold the tarmac in place.'

Cross words chase cross purposes.
Couples' uncouplings
stall, heartscalded.

Settle in front seats,
ignore damp ignition,
jumpstart your engines.
Don't stray down wrong turnings,
chicanes and roadworks,
follow signs for byways.

Holding the junctions steady,
remaindered romances
embedded in tarmac
quieten traffic,
smooth out sliproads,
skim to happy endings.

In the Museyroom

The card reads,
Smell: has it been used?
Close your eyes and breathe
from the neck of the milk gourd
filled by Kenyan cows
a whole wide world away.

Musky warm turf ash, peat-smoke and butter,
Grandfather's house in County Laois.

Deal table, flagstones, delft on the dresser,
apples and bantams by the lost canal,
the deep spice of his felt hat, new every year.

His photographed stare.

Liminal

At this airport where I do not speak the language,
going through security
means surrendering possessions
to conveyor belts, watching them disappear,
standing empty-handed like a suspect,
arms out, legs wide,
while a frowning young official in epaulettes
presses her hands over me,
surveying every fleshly facet,
confirming my substance,
turning her head a little
to listen for dangers
as deer scent the wind.

But I have readied myself for her,
put on body armour
of morning shower and scented lotions
like that old TV ad for deodorant –
Are you nice to know?

She rises from her knees, her jacket gapes,
air is displaced around her, and I catch
the shrill taint of body and soul
maintained in daily struggle,
a working uniform shut up between shifts
in a stuffed wardrobe in a crowded flat
in a flaking building in a city on the margin
of a state in transition
in the difficult confinement
of the historical act.

The Nervous Flyer's Companion

Try to sit beside a boy whose feet have grown
four shoe sizes in half a year.
The in-flight movie will delight him,
and his quiet laughter under headphones
will keep your plane afloat,
dreamlike above clouds, following the planet's curve.

You can watch him take out his pencil case,
flip down the seat tray, draw a cartoon story,
aliens disembarking from rope-laddered spaceships.

Ask to read the comic verse he wrote.
It can be your talisman
as you're shot through the upper air
packed in a metal casing, a fairground ride
where you queue for days and they have to search your shoes.

A Change of Scene

Breakfast in a strange country –
strange coffee, strange milk.

The sun lights on a different spot
on the revolving globe, the names and colours
of a strange town with its own way of going.

Music is sounding in this place
where we are now, eating surprising bread,
watching strange birds, adapted
from the kinds we have at home,
at play in the slightly variant trees.

Counting Children

The little boy is counting, in clear-voiced German,
eucalyptus cones that drop, pock pock,
on the café tables by the coach-trip basilica,

just as up and down the half-mile staircase
to the hilltop chapel with its cold-drink stall and cats,
every child that passed was counting,
in the languages of Europe,
how many steps.

An idle afternoon is stored, recessive,
a hundred aromatic seed-bells saved in a bag.
Picking the crayfish off his plate as a puppet,
speaking its words, snapping its claws for his dad,
he lays down love in his bones like calcium.

The Cure for Earache

English misses its singular word for you
      whose body is a bed of thyme and mint

Let me take off every stitch
      and roll around in your scent

Half-asleep I reach across the pillow
      to touch your bog-cotton hair
inhaling you steadily through my skin
      closing eyelids to the noisy sky
ignoring tactless clouds scudding past

When pain was squealing in my eardrums
      and paid no heed to medicines
your heartbeat silenced it

Multiple Occupation

They have the builders in but no-one's there,
so here I am now, pressed to dusty panes,
gawping at the ghosts of knocked-through rooms.

A new expensive kitchen's been installed
across two households in both downstairs flats.
All smaller now of course. The past does that.

I'm staring through the ectoplasmic fog,
recalling faded rugs and threadbare chintz –
and who are those young people with our names?

A gloomy bedstead that came with the place,
a mattress picked up cheap from a small ad
and carried through dark suburbs on our heads.

We improvised first scenes of marriage here.
Our voices linger in new-painted walls,
our bodies' dialectic and our fear.

Our Own Good Time

We wake to white-out, windows blinded
halfway up with snow.

Clean shapes fur the gardens,
the hushed impassable roads.

All of us in the snowbright house,
power cut and fire lit.

As nothing can be done
we do nothing together,

having hours and tasting them,
minutes bursting on the tongue

like chocolate truffles, citrus,
handfuls of raisins or basil.

Snow time for saving and spending,
and for stealing like kisses.

Fertility Guidance

(for the man of my dreams)

At last we can discard the apparatus,
all my births finally controlled.
More than thirty years of strange-but-true
contraceptive struggles line up for overview.

Hail Doctors Rock and Pincus, hormonal heroes
of space-age cachous tested in Puerto Rico,
pills here disbursed by tartan-skirted ladies
keen that the betrothed postpone their babies.

These blister packs are calendars with omens
of all mortality. Everything turns to grey.
Romeo, every morning I drink to thee
but get tired of the tomb eventually.

Then the young man in the surgery gets stuck
fitting a Dutch cap over my womb's airlock.
One hell of a vacuum on some of these things,
he says, fingers trying to hook the sputnik ring

of the alien dome still docked inside of me,
a good job apparently. If only I needn't stay
while he practises his obscure measuring
and the clinic helper asks again about my wedding.

The trick of insertion makes a UFO
cigar-shape of the thing, which springs in place
and later, squirting spermicidal goo,
I'll fix this membrane between me and you.

Dalkon shields shaped like dinky-toy
stealth bombers, magnified head-lice,
banned from female flesh, go on to boomerang
into some Black Museum, baring their fangs.

The history lecturer says that World War One
'preservatives' were Dreadnoughts like the battleships.
Oh, careful love! Butterfingered apprentices
in hammocks and in beds avoid near-misses.

Today, school kids pass condoms round to check
whether this chewing-gum is really tough.
Now they can be mentioned on TV,
dodging death's virus adds respectability.

Children come home to chatter over tea
of devices they've been shown to plan their family,
latest inventions. *Have you seen a Femidom, Mum?*
You could carry a week's shopping in one.

Blessings on the generations yet unborn;
we who have slipped out of range salute you.
Have all the babies you want, baskets of babies,
and may your safe playtimes be strewn with daisies.

Sprung

Say the children came back to our house
        in the shape of cats.

A whitefoot tabby and a marmalade tom kitten
        stretching on the sofa
prowling the kitchen
        springing round corners
rippling slicked fur
        from clawed pads to arched tails
lapping up
        our fascinated handling –

these creatures
        who made their home with us.

Confused

Sure still of her words, she testifies.
There is a parallel universe in the hospital.
At seven in the morning people come
who shouldn't be here at all,
the sort who attach themselves to a going concern.
She sees them dress as clergymen and nurses,
some with clip boards, trolleys.
Nobody will believe what she has known.

Night nurses with the gliding walk of nuns
come in and out of walls
in the dim nights of the ward.

The opposite bed's a theatre,
the curtained show so wonderful, a spectacle!
The woman there must be an actress.

Her husband has conspired with medical staff
to change her bedroom to a hospital ward.
He has converted their home to a new use.
Six strange women are in the other beds
when she wakes to find him gone,
upstairs perhaps, where he can't hear.
Her house is not her own,
and he never listened.

Where is her life? They bring her home
in a wheelchair for an afternoon,
show her the cherry tree
outside her bedroom window,
the old pink carpet.
She says it is the same room,
but she knows the other thing is also true
though she doesn't know how.

Mind

On the left side which the strokes had paralysed,
a big square bandage hiding half her face
left her mouth free for chat and smoking.
She declared it hardly hurt at all.

A fellow smoker held the lighter,
misled by senses faulty as her own,
pressing his thumb down for the tall blue flame
that melted skin on brow and cheek and eye,
and lit the fall of hair as she leaned forward
like a starlet in a nineteen-forties film.

But while her shriek brought nurses running
she turned to pour the water from the jug
over her burning head. She said
didn't we think that showed
remarkable presence of mind?

Closely Observed

It seemed she died in a very slow train crash.
It lasted seven years
from the announcement of engine trouble
to the eventual derailment.
We were all on board in various carriages
throughout, some of us at times
favouring the restaurant car, or
negotiating set-down and pick-up
at halting places between stations
where the landscape switched on points
from slate to granite to limestone
and toilets could be drained out of sight.

Tannoy messages came in several languages.
Everything was done to keep her going
until the bang came and we watched our mother
bumped from side to side in the smoke
and blackout of the unpredictable moment,
thrown from the buckled door
down an embankment, as the rest of us
tracked on past the scene and the noise
slowed until emergency services
arrived with torches and reflective jackets
for the long salvage and investigation.

Poor Yorick

It's more like that here
     where the gravediggers went to school with my brothers
and the hole they dug was for our mother
     where the funeral musicians liked her
and the priest came to the house for her
     the young undertakers carried her
and her body lay at home in the dress we chose for her
     in a room her grandsons cleaned ready for visitors
and boxes of sandwiches from neighbours
     fed three days' worth of people at her door

On the television people die in foreign countries
     the voice says some scenes may be distressing
they lie on streets under scraps of clothing
     and families weep as the dead are gathered
into rough shrouds and home-made coffins
     carried in a crowd of mourners
howling mouths wide and screaming
     thumping their breath out of their chests
requiring all the world to see
     what has happened and who is missing

It is more like that here
     than my brother's boss across the water
who said *I hear you're sad your mother's died*
     well nothing that a day's work won't make better

Lupins, Later

Again this year blue lupins flourish
their white-tipped spires below the apple tree.
She called pink lupins commonplace,
the blue ones rarer.

Each dappled apex I long to report
to her, held in memory's freeze-frame,
fixed in her wheelchair beyond
the nursing home's glass door,
looking out for me, a daughter,
outdoor air caught in my hair.

At sixteen she believed that babies
burst from their mothers' navels,
unseamed with a soft dry pop,
like lupin pods in summer.

Primary Source

Our mother's womb is buried with her.
O modest collapsible organ!
She held onto it for eighty-three years.
You could say it shared her life.

Perhaps at first she hardly knew it was there,
only heard the word while praying –
Blessèd is the fruit of thy womb, Jesus.

When she found out what it was,
she protected it from the nuns
and their talk of sequestering it
among themselves, and prayed instead
for the grace of a good Catholic husband.

Married, she brought her womb
shyly to doctors and cried every night for a baby.
Old besoms sneered at her small waist –
did she love comfort instead of God?

What arcane rites did they imagine,
she protested, decades after
five people grew from specks inside her,
spinning new worlds from her womb's resources,
taking turns to emerge into their own myths.

Sightings

1. Gooseberry

I shout to him across the hospital bed
echoing her final pillow talk
for his deaf ears, her narrowed breath
demanding simultaneous transmission.
Oliver, I love you, Oliver. I want more time.
I want more time with him.

2. Elsewhere

His path's a slide
of algal bloom he can't make out,
between the smoke bush and the heather.

Behind half-shuttered blinds,
windowed by electric light,
he peers at his computer solitaire.

The garden's shaking,
the boogie woogie bugle boy
amplified to wake dead wartime yanks
who halted in Lurgan at attention,
the whole squad saluting
that shy schoolmistress, her coat open,
walking briskly home –
his girl.

My key rattles the stuck lock.
His ears are tuned to nineteen forty-four.
He cannot hear
the footsteps stop or the door open.
His chair swivels. He blinks at my kiss.

3. At a Garage in Enniscorthy
Off the back seat

eighty-four and barefoot
on the concrete darkened with spilled poisons
no need for a stick yet

he walks

with a toddler's roll round petrol pumps
palming his filled pipe past signs
forbidding smoking on the forecourt

he leans in

to the next family queueing in their car
resting elbows on the father's sill
without a thought of distance

he explains

we're homing northwards from the Fishguard ferry.

4. Holdfast

My mother's waiting at Rossglass, she's still in motion
along a scribbled tide-line in the wind,
a banner of ruffling kelp hoisted above her
to fly out as she runs forever and I look back
forever, with a child's surprise, and catch her face
lost from us in another element, her fist
gripping that live stem, fearless, headlong, rushing
to some far place we did not know she knew,
urgent as a seal-wife for the deep.

The Catholic Graveyard in Armagh

Five in the morning, pulled from sleep,
alert for my nightly after-life review.
Here comes the siren, whoo, whoo,
to rattle the dazed heart.

Now the compulsory flashback tour
of the raw trench where I left my mother,
wearing her navy dress as waked at home
among chrysanthemums, china cups
and a murmur of rosaries in her own back room.

She's two plots away from a newer burial,
the tidiest grave in town.
Fresh flowers always, though it took a year
to find a murdered lad the gunmen hid.

In her neat suburb of the dead
I need no A to Z –
killers and killed housed side by side
when booby trap or bullet
levelled them with their last breath.

Neighbours in sequence are addressed
as if they live here: Mrs So-and-So?
Third on the right. The sister and the father
under their slab in the new vernacular,
polished black marble, inscribed in gold,
carried from China for twelve weeks by sea.

Weeds came up over her while my back was turned.
Geraniums from Cemetery Sunday,
candles in plastic holders and a varnished cross
maintain old decency 'til granite
can name her true and final death.

Visiting Time

I turn off the engine,
take off my driving glasses,
in darkness hug the steering wheel,
let my head sink on my wrists.

Standing to push my arms into my coat,
my back stiffens. A grey shadow waits
at the hospital door.

Now I must know it is my father,
his eyes so old
perhaps he has not noticed
the terror of this moment,
my collapse in the driving seat
like a casualty
of traffic, of family, of age.

Cloudily he stares ahead,
leaning on his stick,
and as he slowly sights me, smiles.
In reflex his arms reach out a little,
so that I am rushed forward and backward at once,
holding the illusion
of being six again
as he leaps over the stream
to rescue me where I have fallen
off the big swing,
my first time trying.

Were he not over eighty and I over fifty
we would run at each other
like any parent and child
playing the game of outstretched arms.

Formaldehyde

Stepping through vacant space
behind our father's hearse
my brother discreetly describes
his health and safety report
on municipal gravediggers' exposure
to deadly vapours
when they shovel shoulder-deep
inside the reopened cavities
of earlier griefs.

Schooling

1. First Year

Facing their questions,
I watch other couples queueing,
but these two look beyond me
to their child's newborn gaze,
her navel cord, her fontanelle,
and hear her midnight cry.

2. Adam and Maiden

They pass to us their envelope of riddles.
Is it sore? What about the first time?
Is it true there are different positions?
And the first people, our first parents,
how did they work out what to do?

You know if they were hardly even human,
if they were apes, sort of,
would ape sex be exactly like human sex?
And would apes need to see other apes
at it before they caught on?
Do you learn how, or do you just know?
Or did God tell them in the garden?

3. Telling the Children

Some faces close on daydreams
because, after all, this is just school,
but eyes that see ghosts look past
the textbook list of Nazi legislation
to scenes where the law insists
you may commit any crime
if your victim wears the star,
has a J stamped in her passport,
and is called Sarah, which is not her name.

Pogrom damage paid for
by fines levied on the injured?
Twelve's old enough to recognise
the lethal slapstick,
to laugh in hope of disbelief.

4. Personal Reasons

After the funeral we sit at home
reading detective novels
that tell us whose fault it all is.

By the shallow pool of paperbacks
we're salted, buoyed,
touching the bottom no problem at all.

Back in school, a small plump boy
explains that he reads *Lost Lives,*
to get into my feelings, Miss.

They learn King's dream speech.
I have to say, *Oh sorry, take no notice,*
this bit always makes me cry.

The child assesses my wet eyes
and says, *Yes, I'm like that –*
I feel, sometimes.

5. Teaching the Unseen

On Fridays I bring you offerings
as if on a brass tray spread with white linen
held on my upturned palms.

A bell rings. We attend to pages
left to us imprinted with voices
human and estranged.
I point to where words sound
across time, how they are held among us.
We invite into the circle of our desks
the living and the dead.

Graffiti Lessons

Where Lurgan is Catholic,
spraypainted capitals some activist
had trouble spelling:
VICTORY TO THE ~~VEIT VEET~~
VIETNAMESE PEOPLE!

On the university bus shelter
in well-mannered script,
Support your local social structure!

The Flush river goes underground
where Lurgan is Protestant:
here and on a banner over Kilkeel
ULSTER SAYS NO!

But in the ladies' toilet
of the Linenhall Library,
Munster, Leinster and Connacht
Say Maybe.

Hand-lettered in leftover household gloss,
red and yellow plaques tacked up on trees
turn the heads of motorists
with threats from God.
After This The Judgement.
The Wages of Sin Is Death.

How long would it take to gather
a shedful of sloganeers
with paintbrushes and fretsaws
interpreting the Word?

Come To Me And I Will Give You Rest.

God Loves You So Drive Safely.

*Beware The God Who Has A Violent Temper
And Never Liked You Anyway.*